Raw

Un-named Lover

It's time I told this story

Before I reach my glory

Wait a minute let me grab the allegory

Scroll through every category

Stored...

See I was only 12 yrs old

How old you were I don't quite remember

Just the dismemberment of my innocence

Once you made that gesture of incest

And insisted to violate me

Though

Your touch so gentle so soft

Only met you once at the time

But I crossed my heart

Hoped to die

That I would never tell

So for years after I sat in silent hell

Leaving expressions and confessions

To journals and poems

But she found them

Banned you from us

But slick-ster mister

You found your way to what you wanted

Until one night that way

Led to my room

And in the dark of the cool summer night breeze

You realized the results of what you groomed

As you entered me...

Father

You always tell me that you love me

Makes me wonder why you didn't fight to see me

Looking into your eyes

Is like looking into the eyes of a stranger

I hate every once you

Very first heartbreak came from you

Feeling of abandonment

I could never have a decent relationship

It's something I've never experienced

My sister and I are a few months apart

Now tell me

I was never normal from the start

You criticize every man

Your daughters are with

Mirror image of you

True

They say women always go for the men like their

Fathers

Understood

But I still don't comprehend the things that I do...

I would love to forgive

Put it in the past

And be able to open up

How to erase twenty seven years...

Possession

Forgive me father

For I know not what I do

Really though

Who am I praying to?

Demons crawling

In my skin

As my sin

Slowly to my end

It's my friend again

You know the one

In my ear

Telling me evil

Can be so much fun

Sadistic

Satanic

Thoughts

Engulf

As I lust

As I loathe

As I lose control

I don't know the spirit taking over me

Yet I understand its familiarity know the vicious

Entangled

With the vivaciousness

I long to let her take over

And storm the sea

Of this galaxy

I am not sanely

A citizen of…

Poison

Poison

Your love is poison

Your attitude is poison

Your personality is poison

Yet I'm so addicted

Like a crack fiend

On the ave

Can't get enough of how you feel

How you touch

But it's too much

Poison

Running through my vessels

Every time I look you in those cold eyes

Poison

In every inch from head to toe

From those braids

Right down to them sneakers

And everywhere in between

Poison

In every word you say

'cause every word you say is a lie

Poison

In every smile

'cause every smile is fake

Poison

Your name is

Poison…

Perspective

Thoughts of you

Are true

To me

Real in every aspect

Yet as fantasizing as it gets

Never the less

I never forget

That you bring

Reality to light

It's out of sight

The way

We fell so hard

Together

And help one another

Up off our feet

Even when see

Defeat as out end

We pretend as if

We were fine

And in good emotions

Damn baby

Some days

You got me feeling

Like I'm on cloud nine

Sometimes

I need to be brought

Back down

To earth

'cause I be thinking

I'm too fine

You always tell me

What it takes

To get me back

In perspective

Your eclectic

Moves

Are electric

Conspicuous

But still I don't get it

Don't grasp

The fact

That your ass got it like that

And oh my

Why

Do you allow me

To continue

This abuse?

What's the use

Of me

Acting silly

And immature

When I know

That it won't

Get us anywhere?

But in any case

Thanks for getting me back in perspective

As far as you get

I've still have felt nothing

What logic is that?

You have the wisdom

I need to achieve

Everything that's desired between us

I lust and trust you boo

God damn its true!

That the almighty

Works in mysterious ways

What made me say that?

Well the only man

That loves me

The way I need to be loved

Is the one I can't be with

Where's the game plan in that

Hand of fate?

Tell me why you're my soul mate?

And please tell me

Where's the perspective

In the objective

You've written on the board

For me to answer…

Dear Journal

Dear journal

This is my confession

I'm releasing

All my anger

And depression

Today he got my hopes up

I thought my family

Was gonna be a family again

But nothing is at it seems

I saw his eyes sparkle

And his face glow today

I am sure he saw that in me

Today I smiled

A true smile

Laughed a laugh

From the soul

Flirted without words

Today journal

Man you should've seen it

Everyone was getting along

Just fine

I was having one hell of a time

But then

His worst enemy

Told us we couldn't be

A family any more

And separated us

That's when the pain

Came pouring down

Dear journal

I know he was heart broken

I was too

We went our separate ways

'cause there was

Nothing we could do

To defend our infatuation

So in this case

 I had to tell my secrets in secrecy

Dear journal...

For Every Moment

For every moment

A word is said

My heart pushes

Rewind

And I submit

The right idea

This time

But never

Was a pause

So long

That I could

End this journey

And be content

With the results

Never could a fairy tale

End with a happy ending

For every moment

A smile smirks

I perk up

And benevolent memories

Console

My breaking heart

Never one too strong to admit

I tried to quit

The indigenous compulsion

But your love urged me

To oblige

For every moment

A thought passes

Never do I be ashamed

For love could

Never survive

Without vain

Just as

Soldiers could

Never be in war

Without pain

For the moment

Our eyes met

I knew my

Life would never be the same

Helping hands

Leading smiles

Always made

My mentality fit

For another day

I knew you'd show me

The right way to love

Issues strung through

Like the strings on a

Guitar

Could you find

The song to my heart?

Jealousy

Occurred in the wrong allies

Made them into foes

Mouths deliberated

Words onto plates

Seasoned with salmonella

And never would I think

That for every moment

You were here with me

It would happen to us

Love separated now

And who's going to hold

Me down

For every moment

You spoke to me

I felt something

So deep within

Fulfilling sin

That made our relationship

Special

Envy

For the void

He could never fill

And for every moment

That I knew you

I was moral's fool…

Mirror

I hate you

My ego's lullaby

You force me

To talk to my soul

Portal to all the demons I hold

The story was never told

They creep amongst the dark

Develop in the subconscious

Depths un-traveled

They remind me of nightmares

With flashes

Of faces I long to forget

Feelings of murderous rage

I long to act on

But I am in a sick

Twisted

Relationship with you

Mirror

You show me hazel eyes

Complimented

Om mastery of seduction

Caramel skin praised

With kisses from the sun

Oh how they want to suckle

Booming lips

Thinking…

Can't help looking like this…

Perfect imagery shattered

As hellish distortion

Sets in…

No self confidence…

2 train in the rain

Battle scars

Battle wounds

Feel my monsoon

Familiar pain

When he nods

To hip hop

I know his story

Our story

Same look in their eyes

Walking in the street

Same rhythm in their soul that feeds off the beat

We both come from the streets

And yet how could another

Soul sista or brotha

Say I am not complete

I'm half the enemy

And so they must compete

But oh only if my heart n thoughts were a mirror

I have struggled the same and even worse

Cuz I am half...

When You Had Me

When you had me

You didn't want me when you had me

Now I'm gone

You say you miss me

I'm so thrown

You we're always the one I waited for

I can't wait no more

You say you cared the most

HUGH... I used to boast

But you turned ghost

I can't rely on your word

To say the words you did…was so absurd

My rib man.. my rib

You were like my rib

Everyone says I'm in love with you

You say you miss me

I say we BOTH love an d miss each other

Our love would die and be for the past

But I can't let that happen

I have to make it last…

You drive me through too much emotions

I'm zoning..I'm costing...

But... I just can't trust you...

The Hand Strikes Twelve

Oh sweet loving hand

Why do you hurt me so

With tender touches

Romantic brushes

It's a wonder how this keeps happening

When I surrender to a corner

And shrivel up into a ball

It's the hand the helps me

Up

That knocks me right back down

Years of this

Delusion

And all I ever see

Are images of you

Improving

Wishful thinking

To gain control over

Blind rage

I witness

The evil

Suck the life

From your compassion

I can see past

The murderous passion

We are a couple of

Fatal attraction...